Excellent

Hotel & Restaurant Service

Why profit is just one reason to provide

Excellent service!

By Stephan Busch

ISBN 13: 978-1546579489

ISBN 10: 1546579486

About the Author

Stephan Busch has also a long career in the hospitality industry ranging from senior management positions with the most renowned hotel and resort companies to the project development - launch of operations, business development- for hotel . resort and cruise companies in Asia, Europe, Canada and Russia.

His expertise includes planning, opening and operating of hotels, international golf clubs, airports, resorts and cruise ships.

He earned his Master Certificate in Hospitality Management from Cornell University, USA and is a frequent guest lecturer at Universities, schools and events for cross-cultural and project management.

Other books from the Author:

Service or War (English Edition – soon to come)

The Yangtze Chronicles (English Edition)

Szenarium 3 (German Edition)

Zum Henker (German Edition – soon to come)

If you are interested in more Cruise ship and hotel stories visit
https://www.itsjusthotelsservice.com/

CONTENTS

-

8. Front Office service
- The digital change
- Reservation
- The forgotten Guest

9. The return to excellent service
- The guest is king – the guest is always right
- Will we change and offer excellent service again?

1. Service in the world today
Service – the opportunity to stage performances

Design, exquisite materials, technical innovations are all part of hotels and restaurants we do not want to miss. And we should always stay up to date when it comes to design and technology. But Hotels & Restaurants without service, without human values are empty shells. That's why I believe that it is important to offer again excellent service on a wide scale. Not just good, not mediocre service – excellent service is what is needed again.

The Grand Hotels of the past were unique places where the owner of the building itself was running the hotel. Today we have managing companies that run the hotel part and property owners. Managing companies can change fast . Today it might be a Kempinski and tomorrow a Ritz Carlton. The attachment to location, the responsibility for the whole is lost.

"From 1960 began the second age of the hotel. The old trade of feeding and watering people was industrialized.

In hindsight two innovations have proved essential. The first was to separate the property business from the business of looking after guests. The growth of debt markets has made it possible to spin off hotel buildings to separate owners, who usually borrow heavily against them. Marriott hived off its real estate in 1992. In 2013 Accor, based in France, became the last global hotel group to embrace this logic."

(1) A short history of hotels - Be my Guest, Economist print-edition icon Print edition | Christmas Specials, Dec 21st 2013

Financially it was a success and lead to the fast development of hotel companies worldwide. It also had its down side and one of the results is the loss of the ability to provide excellent service on a wide scale.

The industrial hotel has been an economic triumph. But over the years its uniformity has made it an emotional failure. Because of its impersonal blandness, frequent travellers have less fealty than pirates.

(2) A short history of hotels - Be my Guest, Economist print-edition icon Print edition | Christmas Specials, Dec 21st 2013

In a recent article that I read the question was asked:

"What is it that is really delivered when we talk about good customer service?

Is it a scripted standardized form of dealing with customers and guests

or

is it part of the intangible characteristics that shape the relationship between staff and customers?"

Unfortunately the growth of the industry has led to a "brand commoditization" that has almost systematically removed the opportunity for staging performances, creating experiences and offer excellent service.

To offer excellent service again doesn't take much. Just a bit of change. This change can not come only from the bottom. It also has to come from the top – the management and owners.

At the end great service can exist even without design, exquisite materials and technical innovations. It can not exist without respect, tolerance, pride, dignity and honesty.

The advantages of excellent service are multiple for guests, owners, management and staff. It is desired by all of them but even the desire is declining as less and less guests know what excellent service is – they simply do not have the chance to experience it anymore or only very seldom. Most guests are already happy to receive any kind of service at all.

The problem is made worse by the fact that our Owners, Management and all the way down to the line staff very few are left who know what excellent service is, how it can be offered and taught and what benefits go along with great service.

It leaves us with a hotel industry that was described by Dirk Dalichau in a rough but to the point article.

"It is a slow moving dinosaur with too many ego driven Narcissistic Managers, who spend too much time fighting ground breaking disruptors such as AirBnB, waste energy protecting their own power, complaining about the demands of new generations and limiting their teams abilities to please guests and deliver amazing experiences. It is full of boring and dated concepts that fail to understand todays traveller and their need for unique and effortless experiences.

Service Levels are shockingly bad due to an absence of TRUST in people. The ill founded belief that employees need to be controlled and restricted in their authority, instructed to follow orders and keep their mouth shut and their ideas to themselves.

Rather than identifying why so many people love new concepts such as AirBnB, they waste their Creativity looking for new ways how to control, and restrict."

(3)   The shocking truth about todays Hotel industry! Dirk Dalichau, Published on July 25, 2016

Lowering the expectations – lowering our standards

The reasons why even only "good" service is hard to find anymore did not start in the hotel industry but in all customer service industries. But we jumped onboard and are drifting into mediocrecy like all the others industries that are supposed to offer service. It is not saving cost that destroys service - it is cutting cost – cutting service. As John Hendrie put it in an article about hotel and restaurant service in 2006:

" We have done a pretty good job with lowering expectations, but that spiral can only descend so far."

(4) Rescue From Mediocrity. The Decline Of Service Etiquette – A Sequel - by John R. Hendrie, Hospitality Performance, Inc. 2006

The airline industry is one example. Before everybody had access to the internet the airlines had the advantage of huge computer systems that calculated the high ticket prices in busy times and offered low prices in slow times. The customer had a ball pen and a piece of paper – and no chance other than to pay. Nowadays the table has turned and the internet calculates very fast the best price for the guest together with the best connections. Anybody flying from Rom to Paris doesn't care anymore what logo is on the airplane. The airline brand has no value anymore. Loyalty cards, Miles programs are only an attempt to put some scotch tape on a hole of a leaking bucket.

How did the airlines, the CEO's react ? Unfortunately the same way that the hotel industry and our owners and top management reacts to the same problem the hotels are facing today.

Instead of demolishing their obsolete business model the airlines tried to compete on price. Be the cheapest on the market and the net. That of course could only work if cost are cut. The service was cut wherever possible. A meal became a sandwich.

Also in crisis the first that has to go is service. At one point during the financial crisis in Asia Garuda Airlines announced that they would cut 20% of cabin staff and 80% of their Maintenance staff. Don't worry who serves your coffee! Worry who serves the plane!

Telephone companies are reduced to the price tag. Service if the system doesn't work? How for this price? Loyal guest that book a hotel room with Hilton only? Why if the internet gives me 100 option at the same location of great hotel rooms plus AIRBNB and other options? The loyal Hilton guest wouldn't have searched before – now he gets it all offered and gets interested in other options.

For a long time companies and customers didn't realize the downward spiral of the price game. Some customers leaving because of bad service ? Nobody answering the service line? Hard to notice. I once needed to chance my flight with Air Berlin and tried the only service number the ticket and related paperwork offered. It was never answered. No e-mail address – no service center. I had to go to the airport to find someone I could talk to and was treated like a nuisance. I never used the Airline again. Now they have lost 50% of their stock value. Maybe it has something to do with customer service?

You should think that at one point the highly paid top management would notice. They should have realized that this can't go on forever. At one point products got so useless because of the missing service that people stopped buying. Where is the value of a cheap airline ticket when the planes are constantly late or cancelled and the food lousy or separately paid for? Who needs a cheap internet service provider when the net is always down? Who needs a cheap business lunch that takes ages to be served and is of mediocre quality?

The result? The price the customer is willing to pay for this services goes down to Zero.

In Germany a customer once posted on Facebook "As soon as my Vodafone contract (telephone) is finished – I will get out and never renew with them!". This post received more than 140.000 "LIKES".

Restaurant service Guidelines to Google

Today the internet provides us with a huge amount of information with a fast mouse click. As much information as for example Wikipedia offers we know not to trust entirely and double check as the information might be partly or totally wrong. This applies to all information and we should use common sense to question and double check as we should do with all media information we receive.

Checking service on the net I get a first impression how bad the status of service must be already. When checking pictures how to set up a table I only find five correct ones out twenty pictures. To set a table correctly is not only done to make it look attractive. It is also done to allow the guest to enjoy service without confusion to make it easy, elegant and comfortable. Setting the table right allows the waiter to provide a smooth service without disturbing the guest and be efficient, elegant and save. If someone follows only this pictures it will result in a wrong table setting that wont even work when you know the right techniques. It leads to frustration on both sides.

Worth is the experience when you search the net on how to be a good waiter. There are titles like

"How to make 20% more tip" (is that the essence of good service?), and tips for waiters like "Don't sit at the guest table, don't touch the rim of the glass, for red wine - ask if the guest wants to serve himself, don't touch the guest ". The list is long and sad. Not only are some tips just wrong. My question is: Are we really that much down to the basics?

The threat of commoditization

This all should worry the big bosses. In the hotel industry we are facing the problem of commoditization. It is the big money game that is bringing the service level down. When Marriot bought Starwood and became the biggest player on the hotel market many wondered how they would keep the different brands separate. Besides their promises – they properly can't. The temptation to save cost by joining functions and departments is too big. It makes sense if you are willing to sacrifice the uniqueness, the service and the individual character of hotels.

Of course reservation system are joined, Sales Marketing and PR and many other functions are brought together to cut cost. The brands get mixed up. The customers are realizing this negative effects slowly but surly.

I got a small climbs of the problem when I tried to book with them. Not long ago I tried to book a table in one of their brand Hotels in Europe. I used their direct web page and already had problems to find their e-mail. I found it and booked sending my mail with all details you need for a reservation - to their wonderful e-mail wecare@(brand No 1).com.

Where – according to surveys - the expected response time of an e – mail is around 24 minutes I received pre formatted answer only 2 days later from wecare@mariott.com (?). The mail was received by a centralized office. Mixes up the brands already but can be forgiven if the request is managed properly.

This mail did not confirm or accepted my detailed reservation request but ask me to specify in which property I am interested in. Meaning that nobody read the mail. I answered and got the next mails (still not accepting my reservation) over the next 2 days – finally after my requested reservation date. Of course I had taken my business already somewhere else. No attempt was made to keep me as a customer. In one e – mail the staff even mentioned that they followed procedures correctly. Of course the staff is not to blame as they follow Standard Operating Procedures and I am sure everything was done by the book. Nothing was done for the guest.

The top management should have reacted long before and should have changed the book.

"Unless I see a brand sign on the door I can't tell the difference," one hotel boss himself admits.

(5)   A short history of hotels - Be my Guest, Economist print-edition icon Print edition | Christmas Specials, Dec 21st 2013

The professionals disappear

Another big blow for service is the long time decline in quality Management and staff. Poorly paid staff makes the hotel industry one of the leading turnover fields. Short time employment , trained with only the basics to fulfill limited tasks. The professionals disappear. Replaced by students or other part timers who want to make the fast cash. They are of course not too much interested to be trained and the hospitality industry is not interested to invest in training of short term employees. An exception is still the kitchen where professionals are needed but they are almost never in direct guest contact.

But it is good that Chefs are on TV shows, stand in the spotlight, give interviews and become stars. It gave a boost to the reputation to the craft and triggered the desire in young people to follow in their footsteps.

But have you ever heard of a great famous Maitre d'Hotel? Can you recall any name? Most properly only if you work in the industry. Why not ? Because it is the essence of their profession not to stay in the spot light. Great Maitre'ds and waiters are there when the guest needs them – and not there when they don't need them. They can read guest, create an atmosphere that gives guest trust and let them become loyal guest. The Guest and his satisfaction will be always in the spotlight. The good Maitre D and waiter will never be. They will never want to be!

"The best hotels, thunders one globetrotting banker, are the ones guests hardly notice. Others like the flattery and groveling but forget who did it."

(6)   A short history of hotels - Be my Guest, Economist print-edition icon Print edition | Christmas Specials, Dec 21st 2013

Sommeliers are the employees that should get the spotlight and this position really did some good for the service reputation. But what would they be without the Maitre and the waiters that organize the surroundings, the smooth evening the balance and communication between kitchen, service and guest, the schedules and the motivation of staff?

Great Wine knowledge was always expected of Maitre D and the good ones are on the same level as a sommelier. But they never wanted to be focused only on wine and wine service. They are the conductors that manage the whole orchestra of a hotel and restaurants, banquets and bars. They are the ones that deliver the whole symphony perfectly that a guest will appreciate and enjoy. They wisely left the first violin to be played by the sommelier.

Management is often not trained but only branded. Little do they know about the variety of services, the possibilities of serving the guest better. Serving the Stakeholders has become the priority.

Of course there are – luckily - exceptions. Those exceptions are mostly in the 5* star sector and therefore out of reach for the majority of guests.

Experience instead of service?

Marketing & PR will try to camouflage with new, now frequently used words like "Experience". The "Experience" is what they offer. This experience also includes the Palm trees, white beach, sunshine, fresh air, the marble lobby. It includes the additional apps, which were either always there or are just innovation of our time that will be a guest demand anyhow. Should this "Experience" distract from the lack of service in the restaurant, housekeeping, Front Desk and in other areas? The "Experience" will do. Yes the overall experience should be great but not be used as an excuse for shortfalls in other areas that should offer excellent service to guest.

"Replicating intimate service on a mass scale is an inherently implausible goal—and when applied to the world's 16,500 posh hotels, the mission has led to an arms race of obsequity. Once hotels competed through their facilities: first came shampoo bottles, then ergonomic mattresses, flat-screen TVs and spas. Now they jostle to engineer "emotional touch points" and "wow moments" with guests.

If industrial hotels do not have an emotional connection with their guests, can they manufacture one? This hope is behind the modern cult of service. Yet perfect service is a slippery elixir: branding gurus speak in tongues to describe it; hospitality professors crunch regression equations to capture it and every hotel chain swears it is what makes them unlike all the others.

Some elements are quantifiable. For example, the best hotels often have long-serving staff (the average tenure at the Bangkok Mandarin Oriental is 14 years) and a happy atmosphere."

(7) A short history of hotels - Be my Guest, Economist print-edition icon Print edition | Christmas Specials

Excellent service should be part of the experience in great hotels. But experience in a hotel or restaurant does not always have to include technique excellent service to make the guest happy. Just honest, friendly service from the heart will do. In simple environments guest will not expect or notice the lack of techniques. Techniques are for us working in hospitality to be more efficient and cost conscious. That doesn't mean that simpler places wouldn't also profit tremendously on mastering techniques though.

A wonderful dinner

I was once in Venice in the Winter. Many restaurants are closed for the season , the weather is cold and rainy , not many guests visiting the city. To find a place took some time but we were successful. Entering a nice, simple but very cozy restaurant full of people we were greeted by a very chubby, friendly smiling Italian"Mama". The first impression was superb. We were shown a table, clean simply set up with all that is necessary. Knife & Fork, a napkin a nice tablecloth ,some olive oil and salt & pepper. Our expectations were met up to this point.

We observed Mama and two younger girls serving the tables, chatting with guest ,smiling and sometimes laughing. The atmosphere was good. Mama took our order of wine and food and continued to serve her guest.

Mama and the girls served fast and tremendously friendly. The only surprise for us was that we were served beer instead of wine. With a look around the restaurant we noticed that we were not the only ones having this issue. We saw people exchanging white and red wines, guest asking if someone ordered this espresso and someone inquiring if somebody received beer. That was us!

Our turn. We brought the beer over and checked with the other guest if anybody had red wine that he didn't order. We found it. The food was the same mix up. Mama sometimes raising her hands to the head and apologizing, guest exchanging plates. People started talking to each other. It was great fun. At the end the conversation in the restaurant was going on between all tables and Mama and the girls. It was a wonderful evening and a great experience. I am sure all the guest enjoyed and – like me – will still remember this evening after all this years.

Technology should only help us – it can't replace us

"Personalized service", "Customized" "Human to Human business" and the "Experience" are recently mentioned when luxury hotels speak about the services their brands offer.

Reality is that investment flows more into marble, technical innovations , design and Golden water taps. Consistent service and long time employees who establish the relation with guest and the hotel – who create the experience - are almost never taken serious or invested in.

The change in Hotel management can be compared to what a stockbroker once explained. The change at the stock markets from humans trading to computer trading effected all sides. When a stockbroker traded he kept in mind the interest of the client who knew the risk but trusted this specific broker and was expecting profits. The stockbroker kept also in mind to maintain a good relation ship with the companies he was trading with. He wanted a long term relation ship trading in the interest of his client. His own interest was of course a factor but he did not want to press everything out of the company he was trading with. He wanted to trade with them in the future and tried to establish a win situation for all.

Computer who trade now more and more and on very high speed do not consider any side. They are programmed to make the fastest, highest profit in the shortest time. Computers do not have principals or moral concerns programed in. If they see a chance to get a great deal they will invest and take the chance even if it means that the trading partner might face bankruptcy or the client might loose his money. The client decided on 60% risk? Here we go! All lost but within the 60%? That was the deal.

"The fish starts stinking at the head", and the higher up the head is, as big as the company might be , the smell filters slowly down. Poor service will effect the profits and until that is noted by the head high above nothing will force them to change. For some it might be too late.

Excellent service exists!

Excellent service still exist. There are individuals , private hotels but also small chains like Peninsula or Belmond – just to name two - that still impress with their wonderful service. But service is a feeling, something subjective that every person would define a little different. The base for excellent service has to be laid so that individuals working in hospitality can fine tune and adjust to the guests they are receiving. They – the staff – will need to possess the skills and learn the techniques to enable them to do so. This is the hotel or restaurant's job and has been neglected for too many years.

I try to avoid as much as possible examples of bad service for my students. Some I have to use to show what might go wrong but there is enough literature listing bad service experience. More important are true stories that explain excellent service. Might it be about personalities that provide great service or stories about service experiences that are hard to imagine for young people but exist.

What are those benefits that might convince our owners, investors and top managers to change? They are in the Stockbrokers world and anything that can not be counted as an immediate or future profit or an assets on the balance sheet seems to have moved beyond their comprehension.

2. Benefits of perfect service

Excellent service requires foremost motivated, trained and skilled staff. Service techniques as well as organizing and planning service right requires professionals. This is an investment that starts slowly paying back but once maintained it consistently pays back over a long time resulting in a constant flow of profits.

Loyal guest.

Guest receiving great service will be loyal. They will return, they will advertise your venue, they will bring their events and functions to your venue. Great service is the feeling of being appreciated as a guest , recognized by staff, establishing relations. This only works with a low turnover of staff. As this guest will have a relation to persons in the hotel that they value and who make the guest feel good. It has much more effect than any loyalty program . This guest is willing to pay more for the service feeling. This guest is not so interested in the financial advantage of a loyalty card. It will be an appreciated addition but not the main reason for the guest to return.

Low operation cost

Once staff is able to provide excellent service the operation cost will go down. The right service techniques – I hardly see them anymore – enable less staff to provide more qualified , guest satisfying service with fewer employees. Two qualified waiters can easily do the job better than 9 part timers that stumble over their own feet , bump into each other , mess the service up, and run around like in a chicken house raising the question in the guests mind if there might be a reason to join the panic.

Breakage will go down and equipment will be handled to last longer. When I see todays dishwashers in action I feel pity for them to deal with the mess the service staff drops at their door step. More dishwashers – labor cost - are needed to sort and clean the plates , cutlery , glasses and left overs dropped of in an unorganized way. More equipment breaks or ends up by accident in the garbage.

The techniques – or the lack of techniques – result in more running for the waiters – again more labor needed – longer waiting times for the guest, unprofessional, disturbing service and more items dropped at the table and inside the restaurant. It has a negative effect on the atmosphere that a designer had thought of a long time and an owner paid a lot of money for.

Low staff turnover

The pride to be able to deliver excellent service in a team of professionals and establishing and maintaining guest relations creates the wish to stay. It goes along with working in a team, good management and a fair pay. Not a tremendously high pay – a fair pay is all it needs. It is an environment to teach and coach young people and create the feeling of a profession with a future.

Reputation

Excellent service will be always be recognized, appreciated and boost the reputation of the hotel or restaurant. Acknowledgment and praise by guest on social networks, mouth to mouth and in media will be heard of. Excellent service is excellent PR and will attract new and more guests. Employees will be proud to work there. Others will want to work there – less HR advertising needed.

Efficient Management & employees

Excellent service organized and executed frees time for management and staff to concentrate on fine tuning, improving, streamlining as well as proper planning and strategy for all departments and last but not least time for guest relation and employee relation. It takes a burden from their shoulders, lets them mentally slow down and their relaxed eyes can focus again on improvements. In many hotels it feels like the manager is most appreciated when he runs from meeting to meeting, gives instructions on the way, and works long hours because without him who would get the shop running? He actually works long hours because he believes it is expected that he works long hours. How efficient he is in this hours often doesn't count. It becomes a process oriented work environment not a result oriented one. And – as the manager is the prime example – gets copied by the staff.

The best managers are totally calm, humble, in control, don't necessary need meetings because they meet everybody anyway during their day and don't work too long hours. They are efficient – get everything including profits and guest and employee relations done in a tenth of the time than the hectic managers. They make things look easy! And that is the feeling the guest should get. Therefor these effective Managers are often labeled - lazy. People who are not efficient and organized can't understand it. It leaves the impression that many of todays Managers, Vice Presidents and CEO's favor the chicken house they have grown up in.

Financial Profit

The summary of all of the above is Profit. There are more benefits like teamwork, team spirit, less sick days and I am sure the list is far from complete. To convince owners and investors profits will be always the number one reason. Important also for employees. Who wants to work for a place that is loosing?

Pride

Pride is important. A guest who is proud to be your guest is all you need. A Hotel or Restaurant known for its excellent service will make every owner proud. Staff – fairly treated, sharing your values and developing – will grow a life long lasting feeling of pride. Pride sometimes gets confused with arrogance, self over estimation – but pride in it's pure form is a value that you share, an appreciation , a bound. Pride in its pure form is a very strong positive feeling that touches people around you. It gives you the same pleasure being proud of a close friend , a team member or a family member. It is a feeling that is easily shared and never forgotten.

Also here some definitions:

Pride: "a feeling of deep pleasure or satisfaction derived from one's own achievements, the achievements of one's close associates, or from qualities or possessions that are widely admired."

Pride: "consciousness of one's own dignity."

One great example of excellent service is the Goring Hotel in London. Consistently providing great service over a century. Stable Management, loyal clients and low staff turnover. Top performance in all departments. Besides room revenue also a top ,record, F&B revenue in a competitive market like London and I am sure top profits . Do you see them advertising or even discounting ? I don't believe they will ever consider this option. They properly have never heard this words. Many people haven't heard of the Goring Hotel either. Some hotels are still so excellent that they can effort elegant silence.

With all this advantages the question remains; what is excellent service?

3. What is excellent service?

Hotel and restaurant service is a performance that requires and combines many skills but also values. It requires knowledge, techniques, motivation, attitude, honesty , respect ,tolerance , etiquette and pride. It is also physically demanding and requires additional skills like stress and time management. It needs professional leadership who share these values. It needs people who like the work, see the value, advance, and at the end it will be great satisfying fun.

The Performance

Sometimes it is compared with a theatre stage performance but I personally like more the comparison with a great Symphony orchestra.

For the orchestra everything is written down – the notes and the times when to play the right note are clear to everyone. The conductor has practiced with all involved, the first violin is ready.

In the hotel the General Manager has everything in place , the furniture , technic and little details are taken care of , the flowers are arranged perfectly , the staff has been hired and briefed and trained now it is time to open the hotel.

Than its starts – both will perform for their audience!

Than the symphony has been played by the orchestra ,

the hotel service has been experienced by the guest

- people walk out from the Concert hall or the hotel whichever of the two performances they visited.

Now they are either carried away by a wonderful experience

or they are indifferent – it was okay

– or worse - they might be even disappointed.

Why ? The same notes written by Schumann or Beethoven, the same amount of musicians and staff , the same instruments and great acoustics.

In the hotel the same amount of services , restaurants , spa , and other facilities in the hotel.

Why are we totally amazed by a concert of an orchestra conducted by Bernstein , Kurt Masur or Seiji Ozawa and are disappointed by other conductors?

Emotions , feelings , positive energy , creating an experience and lasting memories are what hotels and Symphonies have in common. A team of musicians or a team of hotel staff can either create the experience from their heard or execute a technic only.

They might play as a team or just pretend to play as a team. The guest will notice.

The General Manager directs his staff with sincere respect, knowledge , feeling – they will share this feelings without words with the guest. Only executing standard operating procedures in a hotel, only playing one note after the other in the order they are written down will not provide perfect service or perfect music.

Brian K. Williams wrote in one of his articles "love is service and service is love ". The art is to deliver this to your audience – to touch them with your music or your service.

A great lesson is the performance of Issac Stern in the documentary "From Mao to Mozart. " Teaching a young technical perfect Chinese musicians how to play not anymore the notes on the paper but the melody in his mind and heard. You hear two different pieces of music !

A great lesson also hoteliers. (https://www.youtube.com/watch?v=vFtDfNxC1pc)

Perfect Hotel service is for the guest when everything just happens. You might not even realize perfect service right away. When you enter the hotel and everything you expected is there. The services you would like to enjoy don't really need to be asked for – they happen to you.

Perfect Hotel service is the sum of all the services a hotel offers. Very soon the feeling that the day is wonderful – or the thought what for a lucky person you are to enjoy this place will occur and stay with you. The employees serving you are not to be seen when you don't need them. You can explore on your own. The staff appears seconds before you might start looking for them. They anticipate your needs at exactly the right time. They are friendly, polite and respectful and you can't help to feel that they really care for you. You feel save and confident.

You will want to know more of the hotel, the services, what other temptations might be here to discover. Once something is not right or just not really what you liked or expected someone competent will appear on your side, reading your thoughts, your facial impressions and body language and will respectfully solve the issue in seconds without you having to look around to find someone to assist.

This is the hotel service you will want to return to and enjoy again. Once you return you will discover that they really remember you. That they still know what you prefer. You feel liked . Your coffee will come for breakfast without a delay or a question. Maybe just the remark " I hope I remember correctly this is how you like your coffee to be ?" And it will be the way you like it ! Served on the table that you preferred last time and that is remarkably kept free for you without any sign that say's "reserved".

Nobody will try to sell you something or force you to purchase things that you actually don' want. Suggestions will appear without any force and tailored to your preferences already. You will feel good to accept and try something new or you might decline with the same good feeling that it does not change anything Your room will have everything you need and in easy reach. You might never see the maid but the room will always return to perfect conditions. It will just happen. You will be discretely addressed d by name – only if that is what you prefer. No server will introduce himself by name. Once experiencing perfect hotel service you will find yourself asking for his name – check his name badge – because you are impressed! You will want to know. And you will remember.

All this services will be solid and honest. The Ritz Hotel saying " Ladies & Gentleman are serving Ladies & Gentleman", will come to your mind. Mutual respect will develop. The employees showing you respect will earn your respect in return. You will be proud to be part of this hotel as you will feel the employees pride.

Consistency is of importance ! Hotel service is only perfect when it is consistent. One day good service , next day bad service is unacceptable. A period of perfect service followed by a period of mediocre service is at the end - only mediocre service. And consistency has to be planned and organized for generations not for a limited time. Mistakes will happen. This is a human business but they will be solved fast, honest and to your satisfaction.

You might also get the occasional, honest , polite "no" as an answer if the request is not in line with the hotel service. You will respect this answer as you will develop the trust that this hotel cares about you and your well being and will not offer less. It will also provide this honest "No" for you as a service.

Enjoying perfect hotel service will leave you with a wonderful lasting feeling and the wish to return and – that is what we really want to achieve - the conviction that you deserve this kind of experience.

Be aware ! You will judge every hotel and restaurant with different eyes from the moment you ever experienced great service And that is what is needed for us , hoteliers and employees, to strive for the best ! We need to understand that the guest deserves professionals again. And that we will enjoy to provide this service with pride and dignity!

For us in the Hotel & restaurant business – it is easy to deliver even though it might sound like a fairy tale to the inexperienced. Embracing the values is all it takes! The rest comes by itself.

Fulfilling Expectations

That's what it is all about! We raise expectations and we promise to deliver. In hospitality we promise service. Service is a word also used by your car dealer, the bank, your insurance and your plumber. It is sometimes overused and abused.

But the big difference is that we promise hospitality. We are considered – and should be – hospitable, accommodating. Making people feel good is our promise. Good food and drinks, relaxation, great feelings, great experience.

Making people happy! That is what people expect from us when they walk through the door and that is what we want them to expect.

Does anybody expect a government office to offer a great experience? Do you expect the supermarket to make you feel good? Do you believe the bank will be very hospitable and make you happy?

They all offer basic services – which are tasks that you need them to do for you - but they do not set the expectation that you will be treated as a guest. They could be more friendly , customer oriented and they sometimes try but they don't have to as much as we do.

And this is what – and not surprisingly - customers accept most of the time. They provide another product and even though service would be nice – do they really have to bother with that ?

You – as a guest properly never go back to a restaurant were the staff was unfriendly. To a bank – if it was not totally over the top - you most properly will. You don't expect friendly service. You want them to manage your account, savings , the life insurance first. You have different expectations - they don't have to be too friendly anymore. You will come back.

In a restaurant or hotel the staff is part of the service experience. In a bank the staff is only part of the service until online banking or a machine can replace them.

The challenge to make it look easy

One Hotel General Manager told me once the story that he had a conversation with a rich entrepreneur who was a frequent guest.

One morning at Breakfast the guest was observing the whole breakfast room and ask the hotel manager how it is possible to organize a smooth running breakfast for 200 people with so many different wishes , demands and expectations everyday and make it look easy.?

We – in hotel business – know it is not easy. We know the hectic behind the scenes, the daily catastrophes, the hard work , organization and long hours it takes. The guest will and should never see or think about it. Only a few guest look and think beyond the border of their table and wonder.

Other services than hospitality are a different story. Complaining to a bank manager or the car mechanic might result in being drowned in numbers, special terms and calculations far beyond our understanding spiced with vocabulary where we even can not guess the source language of these words. Most customers will not even consider to complain. Believe me - most of these managers do also not understand what they have just told you. They only know that as a result of their speech you are again a willing quite customer. He is the expert – what do you know?

They are specialist! In hospitality the guest doesn't need to have special knowledge. We offer a service and task that everybody has to do at home too! What does it take to get a five minute egg done? Water, heat ,an egg and five minutes. So why is it not at my table after ten minutes?

Many years I was managing a big event in Germany. Up to 50.000 Guest a day , multiple food and beverage , entertainment and VIP areas and up to 900 employees. It took a lot of organization, planning , fire fighting and long hard working hours, little sleep and painful feet to make it run smooth. The first year was the hardest like everything new but it ran smooth and profitable.

After running the event for eight years we had it organized better each year, streamlined , the staff knew the routine and it became even more profitable . The guest were happy and once it was in full swing – at the peak times, we had to watch of course, adjust a little here and there and only look for signs of possible problems and errors that might disturb the work flow. The long hours and little sleep remained. Besides this we had more time talking to staff and guest and entertaining. Some friends of mine who came every year as guests because they enjoyed it so much told me one day that they really think that I am actually doing not much besides talking to guest. The job looked so easy that they honestly believed that they could do it too, without any problems or doubts.

Everybody in our business can imagine how much it takes every time to get it done right again and again. This conversation showed that we had done it right. Everything was great and looked easy. The sweat behind the scene, the pain in the feet, the rings under the eyes were not noticed! That is hospitality.

Sometimes guest expectations are higher than you think.

When I was a GM I had one day a lady arriving and checking in at the Front Desk asking where her luggage was. Normally you expect your guest to arrive with their luggage. I asked her carefully (you have to find out what this is all about first) when did she see her luggage last ?

"Well , your company staff put it on the check in counter belt at New York Airport"! (We had this service up to the check in counter at some airports to make it more comfortable for guest.)

Careful question from my side :"And when you arrived here in Beijing at the airport – did you see your luggage ?"

"No why should I ? You put it on the belt , you might as well pick it up, right ?"

"So you did not pick up your luggage and went through customs with it before our staff could take it?"

"Young men why should I do your job ? I am here and my luggage is not – is that what you are telling me ?

"Sorry but are you aware that we can not custom clear your luggage ? Every passenger has to take responsibility for his own luggage and its content according to airline and government regulations."

"So you really tell me that you can put it on the belt but you can not pick it up?"

This lady expected more service than we were able to provide at that moment. We managed to get her luggage later of course but she never forgave me.

4. Excellent service not only for the rich and famous!

Don't put the barriers up again!

One great achievement of hotels today is that the barriers have been removed so every guest feels confident to enter a hotel and explore. There are of course great cultural differences in the world but in general our services can be enjoyed by everyone today. And everybody feels more confident to do so.

This was often different in the history of service. We still had and have a class system in Europe like it exist in Asia and America. It changed from Aristocrats and peasants to bankers ,politicians, high tech and social media millionaires and a lot of people who's parents left them a fortune. Hoteliers can live with this change.

Affordability was of course also one reason to shy away from an excellent hotel and restaurant. But after the second world war a middle classes started developing , people could afford more holidays , a better life style and could spend more on themselves. This allowed the restaurant industry to develop, the rise of the cruise industry and also exclusive spas and resorts are profiting from generations that are willing to spend more but want value for money.

Danny Meyer, the CEO of Union Square Hospitality Group is an example of holding values high, believing that true hospitality can be offered for an affordable price to a wider audience.

"Taking Hospitality to the Masses

With several successful fine-dining establishments under his belt, Danny said he wanted to test the idea of hospitality in an affordable restaurant, and eventually Shake Shack, the burger joint that's sweeping the nation, was born. The long accepted norm was that great hospitality was reserved for elite dining establishments. Danny proved that wrong by applying the same fundamentals to Shake Shack as he did to Gramercy Tavern, he focused on employees, guests, the community, suppliers and investors. In that order. In every restaurant he opens, he focuses on employees first and investors last because happy employees will undoubtedly deliver long-term results for investors. And with Shake Shack, he has proven that hospitality works at every speed and every level.

In customer support operations, the better you treat your front line staff, the better they will treat the end customer in their interaction. For this reason, we at TaskUs put our employees first, even before our customers, because we believe in the same principal that happy employees deliver better results for customers."

(8) The Hospitality Gene & Why It Matters. Published May 1, 2017, Jaspar Weir President at TaskUs

My Mother would have never entered a top hotel. A 3* star hotel would already have been scary. A 5* star out of the question! We were lower middle class – to put it nicely. Top hotels were for the others. When I started as a waiter apprentice it was accepted. That was my place in life. To serve. Already in my last year in school I was looked down at. A waiter? A Server ? My classmates started their life far up, in banks, insurances , as carpenters and car mechanics. But a waiter? Serve other people? To enter a hotel as a guest was something you saved for the holidays. A hotel that was catering to your standards. To enter the business hotel in your own city was unimaginable.

The classical set up in Germany was that a hotel that had two restaurants had the "City

Restaurant" and the "Hotel Restaurant". The city restaurant had an entrance from the street where the hotel restaurant could be only reached by passing through the hotel. The second one was by no means only for hotel guests and was used also by business and family diners . But the barrier was higher. It was also the place where the aperitif was first taken in the bar or the lobby before continuing for dinner. The "City Restaurant" was normally more casual even though quality was of the same standard as service staff and the kitchen was often the same.

The barriers have been lowered and that is good. More people feel confident entering a hotel of high standard. And we changed the entrances too.

As Guests were scared and unsecure that they might not know the etiquette or the proper way of behavior or simply the use of the right cutlery most hotels adjusted and simplified the procedures and became more casual to be attractive for a wider audience.

Unfortunately standards were lowered and lowered up to the point where you did not need professional waiters anymore but only people that managed to get a plate to the table. That lowered the payroll as for people who only need to carry a plate you don't have to pay much. At first it looked like another plus on the bottom line. Most top managers lacked the vision to realize that they just speed up the downward spiral.

Not everywhere. Some hoteliers realized that lowering their standards would effect the existing group of guest and instead of lowering their standards invested in lowering the barriers by design and education. Education of the guest!

One important high value part of excellent service was available that they could use right away to their advantage. A real professional Hotelier, Maitre'd Hotel ,Receptionist and waiter will not only make you feel welcome he will also make you feel confident , safe and guide you through the obstacles that excellent service might provide for guest who are not so accustomed to it. They will never allow you to be embarrassed. The guest will hardly feel it, no shame and as a side effect a feeling of trust and maybe even loyalty will develop.

But this can be only done by a team that holds the true values of excellent service high and – even better - are trained and experienced professionals. Supported and guided by their leadership - Managers and owners.

With the unfortunate –now long lasting – history of lowering standards we hardly have qualified Management that know the basics of excellent service. How can they lead us back?

Would your small little Restaurant in your home town benefit from Excellent service?

I ask this question a lot. The answer is too often, "NO". For what do we need excellent service? They just don't know what it is. That it can be simple, enjoyable, affordable and also stunning.

Ask yourself as a restaurateur what would my guest like and appreciate? What would make him come back, become loyal? Would he like the friendly welcome? The recognition as a repeat guest? Being addressed by name? Let to the table that he prefers? Suggestions tailored to his preferences? Would he like his service fast and efficient because the waiter knows the techniques and has the skills? Would the waiter realize that you are in a hurry , angry, moody and treat the guest so he can calm down , be served fast according to his needs?

Of course it would be great! What different does it make if you are in a 5* star hotel or the local restaurant? People want value. It is our responsibility to show them what values there are. If somebody drives all his life a Volkswagen and says he doesn't need any other car experience and you let him drive this nice Maybach? Would he feel the difference ? He wouldn't buy the Maybach but he will have the desire to do it again.

Don't over promise. Offer and deliver

In a small Vietnamese restaurant that catered mostly for Staff and students of the nearby University the lunch was very low priced, tasty, filling and served fast and friendly. The perfect business lunch for a short break. They had mostly frequent customers that also joined their bonus program. Once you joined every 7th Business lunch was free. One day my wife - who is one of the frequent customers- realized that she just paid for her 6th lunch so the next one must be for free. She liked the restaurant appreciated the value she received but she was somehow not feeling comfortable asking for something for free. To her surprise the waiter who presented her the bill for her 6th lunch reminded her friendly that she will get the next lunch for free. She was impressed but still when she came for her 7th lunch she did not feel up to asking for the free lunch. She was already happy with the service received. When the bill came the waitress that was working on this day informed her nicely that this lunch was on the house as she was a valued frequent guest. Now all of this was highly appreciated, delivered with the help of some apps that reminded the staff on the guest status and delivered in a friendly way, confirming without a doubt that they live up to their promises. That's service!

Once you know how difficult it is to make profit with a restaurant you want this great service to have return guest. You want this excellent service because it saves you tons of money in the back of the house and takes a lot of tensions out of the team. It creates a wonderful relaxed atmosphere for both – guest and team.

A brief simplified History of service - from Slaves - to the French revolution

The history of service is long. Since ancient times whenever a community grew bigger someone needed service and thus service was organized and provided. There were different ways to do so.

Servants were appointed and sometimes hired. The Romans and the Greeks had the service of slaves as well as the Mayas and the European Aristocrats, as well as most countries in their history. Slaves served in households as cooks , servers cleaners and any function that was needed. They also served as administrators , artist , architects, farmers and secretaries. Any function and any labor needed could be filled with slaves.

Some even got paid and some had the change to buy their freedom or be freed by their Masters will. Up to that point they were the property of their Master. Freedom for excellent service was possible as well as death for minor mistakes or just the Masters mood.

Over centuries and in places where no slaves were allowed or available other servers were hired as maids Cooks and cleaners for rich people and households. Poorly paid mostly and often poorly treated.

This part of history is one reason that puts a negative label on Servants and Service. Key words that leave a bad impression: Slaves , property of their Masters ,poorly paid and treated. A two class system – servants and masters.

In 1789 the French Revolution came and from one day to the other the French Aristocrats fled or were killed and thousands of Cooks , servers , cleaners were suddenly free. Unfortunately – also unemployed and without an income. As bad as life was before as a poorly or none paid servant in an aristocratic household ,at least they were fed and taken care of. Not anymore.

Soon the good Chefs opened the first restaurants in France. Good servers they had and they started charging for a meal and a dining experience. Here the golden age of service in the Hotel and Restaurant industry started. They started as there own Masters – with pride and dignity – as free people who choose to serve . Not much choice as this was what they were trained for – but they knew it to perfection – now they could offer it for their own benefit , for the benefit of a much wider audience.

Cesar Ritz and Escouffier combined Hotel accommodation with first class restaurants , Banquet possibilities . Facilities followed with in room toilets as a start. This period of time from the French Revolution until the second world war was the golden age of service. Of course the very rich could afford it first but it filtered more and more down to the upper middle class and even middle class so they could also get into restaurants and receive good service.

In Russia , after the Russian revolution, it went the other way around. Where in France and Europe a business world opened up where free Chefs and Servers advanced and provided excellent service with a growing pride, profit, dignity and many creative culinary and service innovations the communist countries did not allow the idea of service.

As in all communist countries nobody was allowed to serve another person – as all were equal (at least officially). Service disappeared totally. This was the same in all communist countries from East Germany , the Soviet Union and everywhere the red flag was waved. Seventy years of communism like in the soviet union left a country that could not remember service. You did not get service in a restaurant, a hotel or even a shop. Mostly you did not even get any goods as there was nothing. And if there was only a little to distribute or sell the shop lady was the nasty master of this left over. She treated you badly but maybe had the mercy to sell you something. So you – the guest and customer had to be nice to her – not vise versa. In East Germany you could have 5 tables from 20 tables in the restaurant occupied and most of the staff standing around but no more guest were let in . First not enough food anyway. Second why should a waiter or cook work if he gets the same pay – no guest - or restaurant full of guest?

If you wanted to find a taxi driver in those times you had to look hard . First – in general – almost - no cars. Second the taxi drivers that existed and were paid all the same by the government were hiding. Of course they were hiding. The pay of each driver was the same. If he drove guest or not. But if he drove guest he used fuel that was hard to get and was better exchanged for other goods than wasted driving taxi guest. The idea of Service was dead.

In the non communist countries in Europe it developed different . Even until the 1980's and 1990's it was a respected honorful profession to be a waiter or a Chef and more and more people could afford restaurants and started to enjoy and learned . But from than on it went downward again to where we are today.

5. SOP's Standard Operating Procedures

Limiting the ability to provide excellent service

"Standard operating procedures are most important for any hotel or restaurant" This is a quote from a CEO that I heard not long ago. I totally disagree. It is true though that Standard operating procedure make it easier for the management of big companies to keep control of a certain standard.

One definition of SOP's:

"A standard operating procedure, or SOP, is a set of step-by-step instructions compiled by an organization to help workers carry out routine operations. SOPs aim to achieve efficiency, quality output and uniformity of performance, while reducing miscommunication and failure to comply with industry regulations"

This definition explains why Standard Operating procedures are limiting hotel and restaurant staff to provide excellent service. They set standards that have to be followed and produce managers that ensure they are followed. The word uniformity should ring some Alarm bells. Where is the praised local experience, the uniqueness of the hotel, the personal service when it is done everywhere the same?

"The uniformity and ubiquity of today's hotel chains may owe more to "1984". Employees speak from memorized scripts."

(8)   A short history of hotels - Be my Guest, Economist print-edition icon Print edition | Christmas Specials, Dec 21st 2013

A guest staying in a hotel will arrange his bathroom amenities they way it is most comfortable for him. The housekeeper will re arrange them when she cleans the room first time the way the SOP's dictate. If not - the supervisor checking the room will notice right away that SOP's are not followed.

In an international 5* star chain hotel a specific mineral water brand was to be used in the rooms. In one country the water was not always available and very expensive. The F&B Manager sourced a local water that was of very good quality , presentable and for a much lower cost. When the new GM joined he of course proudly spotted this mistake and ordered to follow the SOP's and brand specification. Of course this resulted in mineral water not being available. The Guest had to suffer as service was cut . But the GM was probably praised by head office for spotting the shortfall in service according to the book. By now the company advertises local, unique products as an experience and maybe they have come back to the product that saved them a lot of cost and satisfied the guest?

The SOP becomes more important than the guest. Of course with the high turnover it is easier to give step by step written instruction that are easy to check. But maybe it would be more beneficial to think about reducing the turnover than spending time to write detailed manuals?

"From Tokyo to São Paulo all omelets must match a laminated picture (they should be cigar-shaped). A manager in Dubai says he follows 2,300 rules, including the phrases used to greet guests. A 2010 Hilton manual stipulates that staff must answer phones after three rings, that guests' pets may not weigh more than 75lbs (34kg) and that scuba-diving boats must provide free pieces of fruit. A 2004 SOP book for InterContinental allows staff to wait until

the fourth ring, requires drinks to be refilled when two-thirds empty and specifies that rooms must offer at least four pornographic films."

(9)   A short history of hotels - Be my Guest, Economist print-edition icon Print edition | Christmas Specials, Dec 21st 2013

Another sentences from our definition that raises questions:

"compiled by an organization to help workers carry out routine operations."

Routine operations should be exactly what the word says: Routine! How can you advance when the worker needs help to even carry out routine operations? Of course in big hotel and restaurant chains that is necessary as the staff is turning over too fast. The Managers are promoted too fast and need the fixed frame of SOP's.

I was fortunate to work in hotels that were top of the notch without written SOP's. The standards were set by the Leaders, Directors, Chief Housekeeper, Maitr'd and Executive Chef and were so high that everybody realized that there is a goal ahead but it will take some effort and time to reach excellence. There was no limit, no ceiling. No standard to meet guest expectations – only the choice to exceed guest expectations.

These standards were followed in front of us as an example. Coached , trained , explained and tested. It was an experience were employees learnt a lot and guest benefited. Especially in hotels the excellence comes from the combination of values ,the ability to communicate with different persons, adjust to personalities and read guests. Of course it needed the routine techniques that everybody learnt first and had in his blood. Like a good dancer who doesn't have to think of each step – the technique , the routine is in the legs and executed automatically. The dancer can focus on fine tuning and aligning to perfection to the music and the rhythm.

This is an inspiring work place where people advance instead of just functioning. It is fun to work.

The following quote is from a recent article by the Corporate Rebels – who I admire for their open mind and non standard approaches.

"Besides having a strong purpose, inspiring workplaces clearly define who they are, how they treat each other, where they stand for and what they are all about. However, they don't bother capturing this in detailed standard operating procedures and protocols. Instead, they establish a clear set of core values that describe the organization's way of working.

The core values are essential for the organization and used by its people as a set of guiding principles. It seems a pragmatic choice because to fully be able to benefit from the collective intelligence of everyone, organizations should get rid of most of the rules, procedures and other bureaucratic instruments that slow down organizations.

A clear set of core values provides employees with guidance to help them to use their best judgment. It provides employees with a framework to act in the right way with the right mindset, without the need of extensive bureaucracy"

(9) STOP FOCUSING ON PROFITS RIGHT NOW!! INSTEAD, BUILD A COMMUNITY ON PURPOSE AND VALUES, *published April 30, 2017, Corporate Rebels*

And not forgetting profits a quote from the same article:

"The strange thing about purpose-driven companies is that the most profitable companies are not the most profit-focused. Various research studies show that purpose-driven

*organizations outperform their competitors. In his book **Firms of Endearment**, Raj Sisodia concludes that purpose-led companies outperform the S&P 500 by 10 times between 1996 and 2011"*

(10) STOP FOCUSING ON PROFITS RIGHT NOW!! INSTEAD, BUILD A COMMUNITY ON PURPOSE AND VALUES, *published April 30, 2017, Corporate Rebels*

The problem in the hotel and restaurant industry today is again that we lowered guest expectations, lowered the educational standards of staff and management and only concentrated on the fast profit. Today we have too many managers that need SOP's as much as their staff. It can't be satisfying for them but how should they know better? In many cases they became Job position 15 that has the corresponding job description 15 and has to follow the SOP's for job position 15. Very inspiring! It is time to show again what excellence means.

"Some of the pitfalls of SOP's mainly emanate from the fear that SOP limits creativity, restricts shortcuts, weakens competition, and denies flexibility. According to EBTE Consultants, the potential disadvantages include that the use of SOP can become more and more restrictive; reduce individual liberty and approach to work; and can become very time consuming; and create a complete controlled environment - ideal for bureaucratic management style."

Is that what we intended? Is that what the CEO and mission statement promises to guest and staff? If it is not – why do we still have Standard Operating Procedures?

Does excellent service need big data ?

The definition of big Data provides the answer:

"extremely large data sets that may be analyzed computationally to reveal patterns, trends, and associations, especially relating to human behavior and interactions."

Excellent service does not need Big Data. It needs small data, individual data.

It needs the human connection. The exchange.

Sales & Marketing & PR need big data and should use it. But they are not serving the guest at the Front Desk or in the Restaurant.

6. A Human to Human business

It is good that this is often mentioned in hospitality but there are a lot of shortfalls when it comes to practice.

I remember a General Manager looking through the guest feedback reports on his computer mentioning to the F&B Manager, " Guest feedback from the last conference were not so good regarding the event organization."

"I know", the F&B said, 'that's what I mentioned to you last week".

"How could you know? The report just came in from head office." the GM responded.

"I was standing at check out and talked to the guests".

Direct contact with guests not only solves problems, it more often prevents them. The same applies to employees. The little talk, the contact is important. It is amazing what you can learn from your guests and employees and how good you can make them feel. It is also amazing to see how badly employees are often treated.

"Smile", is an order, an advise, a rule that is always given to front line employees. Did we give them a reason to smile? That is a question that we forget to ask ourselves too often.

What makes people looking forward to go to work? Money is for sure a reason but more important is to create a workspace, a working environment where people feel comfortable and happy. It can be hard work, it might be long hours like in hospitality but if people enjoy it this doesn't matter. If I need to convince myself to go to a work that I dislike with the reason that it pays me well it won't put a smile on my face. It will make me look on the watch and hope it's soon over for the day. The guest will feel it, the co workers will feel it.

Salaries, Bonuses, Gratuities - Great benefits often turned into tools that prevent excellent service

Salaries

As mentioned before salaries should be fair. That it is difficult to make profit in hospitality also your staff understands. They will be reasonable as long as they can see other advantages like the environment or education that will benefit them in the future. But they also have to live and buy food or shoes for their children. Only to work for a great name, for prestige does not fill your stomach. A couple of years ago even the service staff of the Buckingham Palace were ready to go on strike because of their low compensation. They simply couldn't survive on only having a prestigious working address.

Bonus

Bonuses are a way to share financial success and motivate your staff. They have to be thought through in detail so it is a win situation for the business, a win for the guest, a win for the employee. They have to be monitored. It doesn't help if the business and the employee make money and the guest gets oversold and ripped of. That would be a very short success story. Concentrate on one bonus a time , easy and transparent to monitor for you and the staff. Funny enough many owners shy away from bonus systems as they have to give something more to their staff. Even though they make more profit themselves it seems to be hard for them to give more.

Gratuities / Tips

A difficult topic worldwide. Too many hospitality businesses use tip to reduce salaries or even not to pay any salaries.

In the US tips are expected and salaries are reduced to a level where the wait staff has to get the tip out of the guest. A model I don't like as in my opinion tips should be voluntary and salaries should be fair. Cruise ships are another example where the guest pays the salary of the staff in tips. Base salaries are often so low and not paid to staff until the end of the contract so they can cover the expenses, flight tickets, should the staff be dismissed before the contract ends. Tips are mandatory and often get charged automatically .

In Germany every bill states that "10% Service charge is included". In many countries this service charge is paid to employees at the end of the month. In Germany this service charge ends up in full in the owners pocket and the staff doesn't see any of it. In Germany there was for many years even a tax on tips.

With all this different Gratuities policies and regulation how should the guest know what to do in what country? To avoid all this problems compensation for staff should be fair, clearly outlined in the contract. Tips/Gratuities should be at the discretion of the guest and not demanded. To avoid conflicts all staff should work out and agree on a system how the tips should be split.

Excellent service will be hard to excel if staff has first and foremost make sure the guest pays for them. Every time a guest comes through your door the first question on the employees mind will be "how happy will this guest make me?" instead of "how can I make this guest happy?"

As mentioned the way we treat staff reflects on the guest. It might be worthwhile to read the following question of a young part time waiter why he should provide excellent service.

Why should I provide excellent service for you ?

"Why should I provide excellent service for you ?

Because you hired me as a waiter?

When you read my CV you saw that I was not really qualified but anyhow - I was cheap – and you felt that I needed the money. If you would have wanted someone serious would you have not been tempted to check my references? Like most hotels and restaurants you didn't want to know. Like with most CV's you would have found out that some of the places in my CV have never seen me. I will work for you 8 month until the next place opens next door and as they will be desperate for "experience staff" I will use your mediocre experience to present myself as more experienced, get a little more money and maybe a promotion. Just added your name to my papers – nobody will call you anyway for a reference. So you expect me to provide excellent service?

Because you pay me? You pay me so little that I can hardly live on it. The food you provide for me is expensive and get deducted from that lousy pay even though it is left overs only. I have to pay my transport to work , pay for parking if I can afford a car and pay for fuel. Shoes ,trousers and shirts I have to buy myself even tough they are for work only and have to get replaced often. The vest and tie that you provide I have to pay once they get damaged or lost for a tremendous price that does not reflect their quality and value. I take sometimes food or equipment from you and I know everybody does but none of us feels bad as in general everybody believes its just fair. You deduct money when the order for the kitchen was wrong? You charge us when we break plates or glasses? So; why should I provide excellent service for you ?

Because you are a five star property ? Well you defenetly charge your guest five star prices but you do not invest any money in training your staff or management. Staff turnover is so high that even the most loyal guest does not get recognized. They still come and you could hear them talking: "There is no place were to get good service anymore. But its still better than in......". That's how you get away with it. And as service is declining more not many people know anymore what real good service is. Expectations get lower and lower and you get away with more. So; how should I provide excellent service for you ?

Because Joe is such a great Manager? Well Joe gets paid a little more than we do but he came up the same way I am working on. He has this general terms in his head and repeats phrases like" we have to exceed guest expectations". He just doesn't know how to even meet those expectations and that's why he can't train us. Another good one is: " Its not just the money you are working for it's the experience". What ? The experience I just described above?

"You should be proud to work here. For such a famous name". Yes? Proud of what ? And why its famous? PR people might understand – your staff doesn't.

"We are all family", another great one. Normally used by companies with more than 5000 employees. Quiet a family! And what a family ! Bad food on the table, no money , no trust , no security, everybody is stealing and the family members are changing constantly. Sounds more like a Mafia family but there at least the money is better.

Another good one from our Management "Complaints are a great chance to communicate and turn guest around" Yes – if you know how or if you have someone to show you. The only thing that turns around when a complaint comes is Joe who hides in the office – no help there. Frustrated guest , frustrated staff. Management comes later and explains how you could have dealt better with the situation and sometimes they will charge you as a staff member for damage done. Lesson learnt?

Get Joes position! Than you can hide in the office. .So; Why should I provide excellent service for you ?

Because there is a great future to be expected? Like Joe's future ? I don't know. Anyhow I have to eat today my stomach cant wait for the future and my landlord only waits until the end of the month to be paid. That's enough future for him. My future with you will be as short as possible."

7. The pillars of excellent service

The challenge with excellence service is that it is a combination that needs coaching, training, guiding and experienced leadership.

Skills can be trained, coached and practiced

Knowledge, service techniques and etiquette can be learned.

How many good trainers come immediately to your mind when you will have to look for a qualified trainer for Etiquette? It is a lot of knowledge especially when you consider all the cultures that you will get in contact with in the hotel business. It is a way to be polite and show respect with dignity. To train young people etiquette is very important and will not only change their appearance but will foster their self esteem and boost confidence.

One definition of Etiquette:

"The customary code of polite behavior in society or among members of a particular profession or group."

(11) Oxford Dictionary

Knowledge of an excellent server includes food, cooking styles, wine, spirits, soft drinks and coffee and tea. Cocktails and new trends. It includes knowledge of the hotel, the surrounding area with its attractions and general knowledge for a short conversation.

Languages, at least English is a must. Holiday destinations with specific markets might require more or different languages.

Nowadays you will need computer knowledge to deal with cash registers and reservation systems as well as dealing with apps and IPads.

Service techniques start with the simple correct carrying, serving and clearing of tables and continuous with work at the table side from opening and serving wine and champagne as well as preparing food at the table side, cutting and dishing plates correctly. There is a lot to learn which makes the servers job more easy, more efficient and looks professional and elegant. Unfortunately service techniques are hard to find anymore. They would return once our owners would recognize the benefits for the business.

I like to teach service techniques but I don't see any sense to write them down. It is only effective when shown, trained, practiced and refined. You can write a Standard Operating Procedure for all the different service techniques – and I am afraid someone did already. It has the same result like writing a SOP how to play the violin without practice, training and coaching. What we would hear from that kind of music is what we see today too often when it comes to service.

Competences can be acquired

Tolerance, respect, dignity, empathy are competences that can develop over time but will require experience and good role models and examples. For excellent service they are essential.

The level of tolerance develops most when experiencing different environments, countries , cultures and people. In hospitality you will learn to be tolerant and you will also learn what is best not to tolerate. After a while you will learn to tolerate more as you will have learnt more.

You have advanced and learnt – you understand more.

Respect is something you have to earn. It doesn't come with a name card and a nice title. If you can not pay respect you will never earn respect. I have very high respect for many housekeepers, line staff, dishwashers and other people working in professions where respect is not expected to be given right away. Also do I respect many people in high positions that I have met and learnt to respect. But I had to learn it. It wasn't given. I know many CEO's, Operation directors that I do not respect at all.

Dignity is something excellent service can not exist without! The picture of the slimy , tip begging waiter is in the mind of many when they think of servers. A real Maitre, Chef de rang will posses dignity and pride without a trace of arrogance that lifts him high above the part timer or want to be restaurant manager.

Empathy & Attitude

Empathy is best explained by Albert Einstein:

"Empathy is patiently and sincerely seeing the world through the other person's eyes. It is not learned in school; it is cultivated over a lifetime."

During my almost forty years in the hospitality business I have lived and worked in many countries and I have learnt a lot. I became more tolerant and respectful and I am thankful for all the people that tolerated me even when I was young, stubborn and stupid. The ones who didn't give up to teach me and to the ones that earned my respect. I am grateful to those who's respect I was able to earn. It gives me the patience to teach and coach today

Everybody has an Attitude. Whatever kind of Attitude it might be. Don't try to train Attitude – it's hopeless. Many companies pride themselves that they hire only attitude and not necessary experienced staff. Why not both? That makes only sense after we now have figured out that the same people who now only hire attitude are responsible that the professionals with great attitude and experience have been extinguished.

9. Front Office service

The front office is often refereed to as the "key", the "First Impression" for a hotel. Its importance is not disputed but it is not more important or less than any other department of the hotel. The "First impression" of the hotel the guest had already before approaching the reception. Reservation, online booking, past experience and reviews formed already the expectations of the guest. Now when Guests are physically entering the service has to win the guest. The impressive Marble lobby is good but expected from the nice pictures on the net or in the catalogue. But what is happening now to the guest? How is he greeted, get access to his room, made feel welcome?

Front Office is where the staff is at the front , the guest reaches the front and it is the first human confrontation in the hotel. Sounds negative? But it brings it to the point. Front is perceived negative as it is also associate with war. But to be in front, leading people in business, leading your family, guiding and coaching in front of your employees is positive. It can set positive examples. A conformation is also often perceived negative. But a confrontation can be positive and productive. A discussion, a Q&A session. A business coach confronting you with what you need to hear. In hotel business we have to express ourselves more positive but we should think clear with clear words. This is how we learn best.

Of course we would not use an explanation like this for our guest. Even though the guests that I knew well enough and had a genuine interest in hotel operations always appreciated when I explained it this way. For our daily guest we would describe Front office where the staff is on stage , the guest approaches and the first human to human contact is established.

There are a lot of so called "Innovations" like removing the reception counter and greeting the guest in the lobby, checking him in in a casual seating arrangement. Its for sure a good idea but not something new as we had this already long time ago in hotels . Some took it even further. I had check in where a staff member greeted me by name while opening the taxi door, ask me if I had a nice trip, told me not to worry about luggage and brought me into the hotel. While walking the offer of a refreshment in the bar was made or the option given to be guided directly to the room. Polite casual conversation , offering assistance, and pointing out features of the hotel. In the room a small card was produced to sign, the room features shortly explained and that was the check in. I never had to stand at a counter (the barrier) , explain my personal details and wait that somebody shows me to the elevator.

On other occasions you feel just processed. Standard greeting for everybody, eye contact or not. The faster the check in – the better! Personal interaction slows the process down.

Of course it sometimes depends also on the price but some 5*star hotels manage to make you feel like you have to be thankful that they accepted your booking. And some 2* star hotels make you feel home right away. In some hotels you realize on entering that the service is not thought through. I entered once a city five star hotel where the doorman opened the door politely, with a friendly greeting and when I entered I had to walk 5 meters towards a big grim looking security guard who stood with legs apart, arms crossed, walkie talkie knob in the ear and looked at me so that I could imagine what will happen if I make a wrong move. When I passed by, I breathed with relief and came to the reception where I was greeted by two nice ladies. Which made it easier but somehow my first impression was not the greatest. I would have loved to see the ladies first.

The digital changes

Another change is of course related to technique and the digital innovation of our time. Remote payment is already a widely excepted , long established option ,but Apps for self check in , Concierge service apps and more and more service that can be processed through devices . This is a good option for guest who prefer to use them. It's not the human to human relation but if this is the guest choice than we should be able to provide it. Important is that we will only see it as a choice. The human service still will need to be provided by humans for guest. The advantage of the apps is obvious. Faster more convenient service for the guest that wish to use them, lower labor cost and also faster processing for the hotel that only has to set the system to make sure it works well for both sides. Hotels with thousand of rooms will avoid long lines on check in and will thus be able to serve their guest better.

The human contact will still be there to connect with guest, read people, anticipate needs and give the human touch and allow for empathy which even in the digital age can't be done by devices.

There are multiple companies that offer digital services and for hotels with a big room inventory it is almost a must today to secure this services. Smaller companies can also profit tremendously but should evaluate which service is appropriate and which is not needed. StayNtouch is one of the popular providers and it makes sense for every hotelier to be familiar with the possibilities they and other providers offer.

Reservation

The last 100 years have seen a lot of changes in the way Reservation are handled. From the time people had sent a courier or a letter to reserve a room are the past. The telephone changed the world again and from calling a single hotel for a reservation to centers that took reservations for multiple properties was a small step.

Today online booking is the most popular way to make a reservation not only for a hotel room but also for restaurants and all other services. Hotels have to keep up to date on web design, search engines and all digital tools available to attract the direct booking guest. This is were professional companies should be involved as the digital world is changing too fast for hoteliers to keep up to date as a side business. The OTA's will be still part of the game and as hotels realize that they have to corporate and live them it might be beneficial . Even though commissions have to be paid OTA's will always fill rooms.

Reservation is a great chance for service. The friendly voice that shows empathy, suggest additional, can up sell should not be forgotten. Of course it is not the most important one anymore – online has taken over. But a follow up by phone for a reservation received, just a confirmation with the offer of assistance and help can go a long way and will be received as great service.

Some hotels started to follow up with e-mails offering easy purchasable or free services tailor made to families, groups or business travellers. From the extra children menu to excursions and work space suggestions. This is also a way to up sell or just be hospitable and leaves the guest with the choice to ignore or take advantage of them. It will be for sure appreciated especially when it is personalized and not just a computer message.

Reservations should always give the guest the feeling of being appreciated and not just simply accepted and processed. Guests have too many options.

(12) STOP FOCUSING ON PROFITS RIGHT NOW!! INSTEAD, BUILD A COMMUNITY ON PURPOSE AND VALUES, *published April 30, 2017, Corporate Rebels*

Loyal guest , may it be single Persons, groups , event reservations should have there own top priority for every hotel or restaurant. Once a guest returns to a place he had a good impression the first time. You can destroy this in seconds not remembering him, treating him like everybody else. Once a reservation request is coming from a repeat guest you have to have a system in place to realize that this is special. Best is of course a person on your staff that has already established a personal connection and can follow up in person. But once your system alerts you on a repeat reservation follow up immediately letting the guest know that you are happy to see him again , offer more assistance make him feel special.

For business reservation it is essential to stay in contact with the person booking. Often it is not the Guest himself. The guest might even not remember you , the person booking will once you meet this guest expectations and fulfilled the expectation of the person booking on his behalf.

The guest would never be with you if it wasn't for this person. It might be the secretary , personal assistant or agent . Special occasions to stay in contact or even invite them can be always found. This people are key to many follow up reservations in the future. They will of course expect you to treat their guest extra special.

In Germany I often stay in a boutique hotel , 5*stars, nice Spa and super Restaurant. Only 30 rooms and the barman and restaurant staff always remember me for many years. But every time I book a room by e mail the questions comes from reservations " are you the first time booking with us? ,How did you here about us?" I am sometimes tempted to tell them to ask their restaurant staff or get a computer system that tells them that I am a loyal repeater.

I remember the business trainers we had in many hotels teaching us classroom style how to keep a record of the guest. Details of Food & Beverages preferences, the table he liked, the room he preferred , the dislike of certain flowers and so on. The amazing follow up was that all staff from Front Desk to waiters scrippeld in notebooks by hand , later by computer big amounts of information that at the end where never or hardly used. We just didn't have the time to shuffle through when the guest arrived and turned to the old employees (who wisely never followed the trainer) to ask them what to do best. That worked and taught me a lesson for life.

Monitoring your reservation you will see the opportunities to avoid a nasty overbooking situation that will up set every guest. In low times you might also see the chance to offer something special for those guest or key persons who provide reservations. When you are not getting the house full why not offer a fantastic price to those and their friends or just invite them free of charge?

The forgotten Guest

The guest that doesn't reserve and book anymore should have your attention. Processing bookings , attracting guest for future bookings keeps your reservation department busy. But what is with guest that suddenly doesn't book anymore? The company that is not using your hotel anymore? Is anybody noticing ? Does your hotel want to know where they are ? Why they are not coming to you anymore?

Following up takes a little time and research but can reactivate guest and bookings that were lost . Maybe a complaint that was not handled right? A personal follow up will give the chance to recover the guest. Maybe your competition captured them? Why? What can you do better? A lot of possibilities for additional revenue. You will not get all back as there are also natural reasons for people to disappear but you will recover some and the service of remembering them, paying attention and contacting them will be appreciated.

For being efficient and successful in Reservation Department technique, digital and all other tools have to be activated and constantly up dated. The human factor can't be neglected as it will back fire if you only leave it to the robots to deal with your human guests. A human with emotions in a happy work environment will make reservations successful fun. A human reading from his SOP's can be an accountant , student, or the cleaner. No emotion needed. Success will depend how good the script is but never more than standard.

8. The return to excellent service

It is my believe that we will see the return of excellent service also on a wider scale. We have to do it for the hospitality as such , for us, and for the guest.

The Guest is King – the guest is always right!

Is that really so ? Are they always right?

I always remember the words of a great Maitre d'Hotel I worked with: "A Guest is a guest as long as he behaves like a guest!"

There are guest that you don't want or need. Guest that are disrespectful to other guest, your staff - disturb or even wreck your business. Do you want them ? Do you want to make them feel being right?

Than ask the other guest and your staff what they think. These guests are a minority but you - as an owner - as a manager - you have the responsibility to protect you guest, your staff and your business. You can only win when your staff and your guest trust you. You have to show them trust first. That means defending them when necessary - respecting them at all times. Trust is one of the most important pillars in business. Trust like respect is not automatically delivered with a title. It has to be earned and gained.

Can the guest be king? What is left of the monarchy are Kings who are nowadays people who only have ceremonial functions in some countries. They might have some influence but no decision power. In most countries they are only history and have been extinguished Does this description has any thing in common with our guests of today?

Will we change and offer again excellent service?

For sure we will and we are changing already! As mentioned there are still Hotels and Restaurants that never stopped delivering excellent service. To offer it on a wide scale again is a change that, as we said before, will have to come from the top and from the bottom.

Looking at the Restaurant sector there are many fantastic concepts and there are always innovative people coming up with new ideas. In the Hotel sector the best in service are the small and often independent hotels. They offer local, customized, personalized service not because they invented this as a new concept. They can offer this because this is what they truly are and always were.

From the big hotel chains we can unfortunately not hope for much innovation when it comes to excellent service. Technical and digital innovations for sure as they have the financial power but for being truly able to offer personalized service the have simply grown to big. They have to rely on SOP's to control their empires which limits them already. For new ideas, concepts and innovations to brake through and being implemented they have to go through layers of corporate offices and approvals. Innovation dies slowly on the way.

It shows when it comes to Hotel Restaurants. Outsourcing the restaurant space is a way to get a safe income on the balance sheet by collecting the rent and not to worry about the F&B related costs. It always amazes me when I see a wonderful successful outsourced restaurant concept in a five star chain hotel. There are many! With all their manpower, all the financial advantages, all the logistical support available could the hotel not come up with a concept like this?

We have to continue to train and coach young people to understand what excellent service is, how it can be delivered and maintained. We have to work on the reputation of the professions and have to manage the benefits better.

All hospitality professions should be attractive again when it comes to showing a path to a successful career. Why do we need more certificates or an MBA or PhD nowadays to get into management? The possibilities for a bride, hard working individuals with the right attitude and willingness to learn to make there way up were multiple in the past. The way up from bellboy to GM was a possibility.

Why do we have so many GM's with F&B background but so few from Housekeeping? A Chief Housekeeper able to manage a multi national workforce and the multiple challenges of this department has what it takes to manage an entire hotel. The additional relevant knowledge of the other hotel function can be learned the same way the F&B person has to do it.

To learn again to provide excellent service to our guest we should look a little bit back. The times when we did not have all the devices on hand that we use now. This look back should not bring us back in time . We have to go forward and under no circumstances ignore or avoid the innovations, the advantages that our digital world of today provides. They are necessary, and good to make life easier , more convenient for our guest and us. But at a time when all this tools were not available service depended only on the human members of staff. Coaching, learning by experience made them perfect when it came to service technique and etiquette. They also could read guest, adapt to difficult situations, had a memory of guests and their behavior which they gave on to the younger ones. Serving the guest best and up selling in the restaurant was taught in stages. Remember what the guest preferred, adjust to his mood of the day, to the company he is in today and to all the influences that may change guest behavior. For new guest: Read the guest, judge the behavior, dress code, is he alone or with what group of people? Consider time of the day, rushed or does he look like he has time? Business or leisure? A lot of questions that after a while you could answer faster and faster. And the better you got the easier the job was, the more satisfied the guest was. And still the old long staying employees could surprise you and show you another twist.

Combine this with the tools that we have today on hand and service can be perfect. Unfortunately we neglected the human part and rely mostly on tools. The guest is still human, it is us who became more robotic. For hotel chains with more than 1 Million rooms and thousands of properties spread all over the world it is the only way to rely more on devices, tools, technique and SOP's to be able to manage. They have to rely on Marketing phrases like "exceeding guest expectations", "the Experience", and the "Wowing" of guest. There were times when we made this happen to guest without having to brag about it.

This leads unfortunately to the younger Generations growing up in an environment that makes them believe it is the only way. For a real hotelier it will never be satisfying. This in turn gives the hope that entrepreneurs will discover this possibility for themselves and continue what still exist in a small niche and open it again for a wider audience. The new generations are the ones that we should encourage to become those entrepreneurs.

"The shocking complacency and lack of drive to change these circumstances is surprising, as the new generations display an enormous sense for values, real mission and a desire to make a difference. They are a significant indication for the future highlighting what both employees and guests will expect. And yet too many people refuse to make changes. They prefer silent executors as opposed to proactive initiative taking team members."

(13) The shocking truth about todays Hotel industry! Dirk Dalichau, Published on July 25, 2016

Most important is to always keep in mind that we have to do it for the guest. Our benefits will follow. The guest has more options today than ever and will explore, learn and be more educated also when it comes to excellent service. The Guest will demand more and better service and we should be ready to deliver.

THE END

REFERENCES

(1) A short history of hotels - Be my Guest, Economist print-edition icon Print edition |
Christmas Specials, Dec 21st 2013
(2) (3) The shocking truth about todays Hotel industry! Dirk Dalichau, Published on July 25,
2016
(3) (4) Rescue From Mediocrity. The Decline Of Service Etiquette – A Sequel - by John R.
Hendrie, Hospitality Performance, Inc. 2006
(4) (8) The Hospitality Gene & Why It Matters. Published May 1, 2017, Jaspar Weir President
at TaskUs
(5) (11) Oxford Dictionary

(6)

ABOUT THE AUTHOR

With more than thirty years in the hotel industry Stephan Busch has an invaluable and diverse experience in the hospitality industry ranging from senior management positions with the most renowned hotel and resort companies to the project development - launch of operations, business development- for hotel . resort, cruise companies and hotel schools in Asia, Europe, Canada and Russia.

His expertise includes not only planning, opening and operating of hotels, international golf clubs, airports, resorts ,cruise ships and schools, but also successful restructuring and repositioning of businesses during the financial crisis in Asia.

Besides launching new complex tourism and cruise projects in Asia and renovation projects in Russia, Mr. Busch has been responsible for the planning, organization and execution of multiple ATP Tennis Tournaments and government functions in Europe and is continuing to organize and manage events for up to 45.000 guests per day.

Stephan Busch earned his Master Certificate in Hospitality Management from Cornell University, USA and is a frequent guest lecturer at Universities ,schools , international conferences and events for cross-cultural and hotel management as well as the Author of "The Yangtze Chronicles" a documentary fiction about the Three Gorges Dam.